REEDS
KNOT
HANDBOOK

REEDS
KNOT
HANDBOOK

A POCKET GUIDE TO KNOTS, HITCHES AND BENDS

JIM WHIPPY

PARADISE CAY
PUBLICATIONS
www.paracay.com

Paradise Cay Publications, Inc.
Arcata, CA

Copyright © Adlard Coles Nautical 2011

First edition published 2011

ISBN 978-0-939837-93-9

Edited by Linda Morehouse, www.webuildbooks.com

Note: while all reasonable care has been taken in the publication
of this book, the publishers take no responsibility for the use of the
methods or products described in the book.

Printed and bound in China.

Published by Paradise Cay Publications, Inc.
P. O. Box 29
Arcata, CA 95518-0029
800-736-4509
707-822-9163 Fax
paracay@humboldt1.com
www.paracay.com

KNOTS • HITCHES • BENDS • WHIPPING • SEIZING

CONTENTS

INTRODUCTION

As soon as man started to make weapons for hunting and to adorn his body with clothes, he needed to find ways of securing items and for this he used plant fibers and, a little later, catgut. Fibers were used in early crafts such as basketmaking and weaving, and man discovered that by tying knots the fibers could be held together more securely.

Man quickly progressed, using knots to build bridges and make shelters and he quickly found more and more uses for knots, until they became a vital component of everyday life.

Sailors, too, quickly learned the value of various knots to secure their rigging, sails, and fishing nets. During long journeys at sea, sailors would spend much of their spare time developing new knots, and some of the original names used by these men are still in use today.

The majority of the knots in this handbook are intended for nautical or fishing use; for that reason, we have used the traditional sailing terms for tying knots:

- *the working end* – the piece of rope currently being worked.
- *in the bight* – the middle portion of the rope that you are working on.
- *the standing part* – the piece of rope that is not currently being worked.
- *the end* – the part of the rope that is liable to fray if not whipped.
- *to dress* – to neaten the separate parallel strands, making sure they are free of kinks and twists.

Most of the knots are tied in rope, cord, twine, yarn, or thread, depending on their intended purpose.

This book is divided into six categories: Overhand Knots and Hitches, Figure-of-Eight Knots, Bowlines and Bends,

Crossing Knots, Wrap and Tuck Knots, and Other Useful Knots. Each knot is broken down into simple, concise step-by-step instructions and is accompanied by clear illustrations and hints to guide you as to when and how to use each knot. With this book you will come to realize the infinite number of uses for knots and learn which one is best for the job at hand.

When choosing a knot you will need to bear a few things in mind:

- the strength of the knot required
- the working conditions
- will the knot need to be tied quickly?
- will the knot need to be released quickly?
- the size of the knot—will it need to pass through an eye, a hole, or something similar?

Today there are many different types of rope to choose from, but they fall into two general categories: natural fibers and artificial fibers. Natural fiber ropes, which are made from plant fibers woven together, tend to feel rough to the touch and appear slightly "hairy." You will find that natural rope is more prone to damage, especially when exposed to sea water for long periods of time, as this can cause it to rot. Natural rope fibers can also swell when wet, which can make the knot cumbersome and very difficult to untie.

Artificial fiber ropes have several advantages over natural. They can be made in any length; they are generally stronger; they can be made in any color, and they are capable of withstanding shock when under load. However, there are also disadvantages, as they can become slippery when wet, which makes it easier for the knot to slip. Artificial fiber ropes are manufactured from nylon, polyester, or polypropylene, all of which give the rope different characteristics—so select with care.

ALBRIGHT SPECIAL

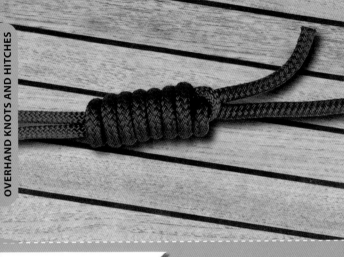

STEP-BY-STEP

1 Make a loop in the thicker line and pass about 25 cm (10 in) of the lighter line through the loop. Now start to wrap this around the loop.

2 Hold the three lines between your index finger and thumb and wrap the line tightly around the loop 7 to 10 times, making sure the line doesn't twist.

The Albright special (or Albright knot), named after an American fly fisherman, Jimmie Albright, has been used for over half a century. This extremely versatile knot gained popularity because it was believed to be the first knot that could be used successfully to connect lines of different diameters—for example, monofilament to braid.

Although the connection is generally firm, you should err on the cautious side when pulling up, as it has been known to slip. If using the Albright special, take extra care when finishing the knot that it is pulled up tightly, especially if you are working with wet hands. Also make sure that the wraps lie neatly and that they are not crossing over one another.

③

Next, feed the end of the wrapping line down through the loop so that it lies next to its other end.

④

Hold the line taut and pull gently on all four strands. Now let go of the shorter of the two pieces on each end and finish the knot by pulling the longer pieces tight.

BOOM HITCH

STEP-BY-STEP

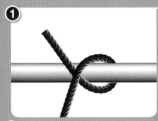

1 Wrap the working end of the rope around the post. The post can be either vertical or horizontal.

2 Bring the working end under the post and cross it over the previously laid diagonal, trapping the first loop under the new one.

The boom hitch is an extremely strong knot that is almost impossible to break. It is useful if you need to attach a rope to a fixed object and works exceptionally well on rounded rails and sail booms. If you want to make it easier to untie, it can be finished with a bight tucked under, rather than the whole line pulled through, as in Step 5.

When other hitches are inappropriate, or if you are unsure of which knot to use, the boom hitch is the one to choose because it remains solid even in exceptionally wet and windy conditions.

An easy way to remember how to tie this knot is to repeat to yourself:

over / over / over / over and finally tuck.

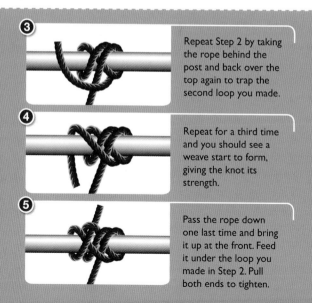

③ Repeat Step 2 by taking the rope behind the post and back over the top again to trap the second loop you made.

④ Repeat for a third time and you should see a weave start to form, giving the knot its strength.

⑤ Pass the rope down one last time and bring it up at the front. Feed it under the loop you made in Step 2. Pull both ends to tighten.

BUNTLINE HITCH

STEP-BY-STEP

① Pass the working end of the rope through an eye or ring and then form a figure of eight as shown here.

② Working from right to left, bring the working end behind the standing part and through the loop closest to the ring.

14

The buntline hitch (effectively two half hitches) is a simple and effective knot that was traditionally used to secure a line to the foot of a sail on a square-rigged vessel. Its reliability is due to the fact that it will tighten rather than loosen when subjected to jerking. This knot is still popular because it works extremely well on the slippery synthetic lines more commonly used today.

The buntline hitch is useful if you want to attach lines to rings, eyes, posts, or railings and when you need to guarantee a secure fixing. One word of caution, though: the buntline hitch can jam when subjected to loads, making it difficult to release.

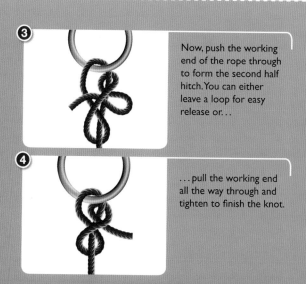

❸ Now, push the working end of the rope through to form the second half hitch. You can either leave a loop for easy release or...

❹ ...pull the working end all the way through and tighten to finish the knot.

DOUBLE OVERHAND KNOT

STEP-BY-STEP

① Tie an overhand knot by making a loop with your rope. Take the working end and pass it through the loop you have just made.

② For a double overhand knot, make an extra turn with the working end.

The overhand knot is described as a stopper knot because it prevents a rope pulling through an anchor point. It is one of the most basic of all knots. It is also used at the end of a rope to prevent it from fraying or unravelling.

It is often the starting point for several other knots such as the fisherman's knot (see pages 22–23) and the angler's loop (see pages 82–83) and is an extremely secure knot if you want something that is permanent.

The overhand knot can be added to by making more turns, and this is then referred to as the double overhand knot or triple overhand knot, depending on the number of extra turns. It is an important knot as it is frequently used in fastening the ends of yarns and strands in splicing, whipping, and seizing. It can also be tied at regular intervals to form a makeshift handrail.

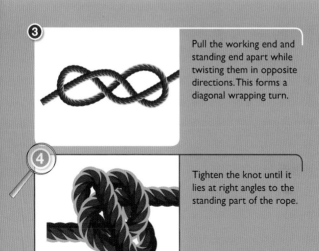

③ Pull the working end and standing end apart while twisting them in opposite directions. This forms a diagonal wrapping turn.

④ Tighten the knot until it lies at right angles to the standing part of the rope.

FIREMAN'S CHAIR KNOT

The fireman's chair knot (also referred to as Tom Fool's knot) is tied in the bight and forms two adjustable, yet lockable, loops. Designed to be used as a rescue harness, this knot is capable of supporting a person being lowered or raised to safety. One of the loops is designed to support the body by placing the rope under the armpits and around the chest. The second loop supports the legs, around the back of the thighs.

Although you will hopefully not find it necessary to have to tie this knot, it is handy to know just in case of an emergency when there is no proprietary harness handy. Pulling the loops so they fit snugly around the person's body allows you to maneuver the rescued one safely even if he is unconscious.

STEP-BY-STEP

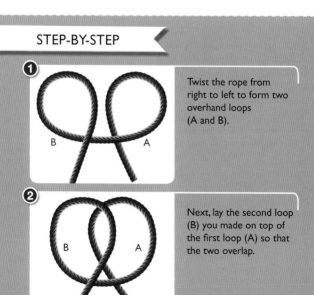

① Twist the rope from right to left to form two overhand loops (A and B).

② Next, lay the second loop (B) you made on top of the first loop (A) so that the two overlap.

FIREMAN'S CHAIR KNOT

③

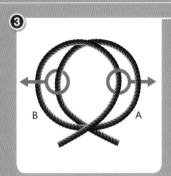

Pull the right side of loop B through loop A from above, downwards; at the same time pull the left side of loop A through loop B from below, upwards.

④

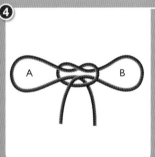

Adjust the size of the loops required—this will depend on the size of the person to be rescued—and tighten the knot.

⑤

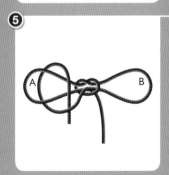

To lock loop A, tie a half hitch, making sure its standing part is around loop B.

6

To lock loop B, tie a half hitch, making sure its standing part is around loop A.

7

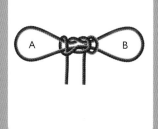

Once you have locked both loops, snug the two half hitches up to the center knot. Pull to tighten the knot, leaving one central knot with a loop on either side.

FISHERMAN'S KNOT

STEP-BY-STEP

1 Take two ropes of roughly the same thickness and hold one in each hand. Tie an overhand knot in the rope in your right hand and slip it over the rope in your left hand. Pull gently to tighten the knot a little.

2 Make an overhand knot in your left hand, tying it around the rope in your right hand. Pull gently to tighten the second knot a little.

22

The fisherman's knot is easy to tie because it is simply made up of two overhand knots. It is most commonly used to join two lines of about the same thickness. You may also find this knot referred to as the angler's knot or the waterman's knot. It is one of the oldest knots in existence.

The drawback with this knot is that it can slip if tied in nylon monofilament or other types of slippery fishing lines, but the problem can be overcome by tying the knot with more turns. In its favor, it can easily be tied when your hands are cold and wet, it is compact, and it's possible to trim the ends close to the knot without it coming apart.

Your ropes are now joined by two overhand knots. Pull on each rope so that the two knots slide along the rope until they are next to one another, which will give you a secure hold.

HUNTER'S BEND

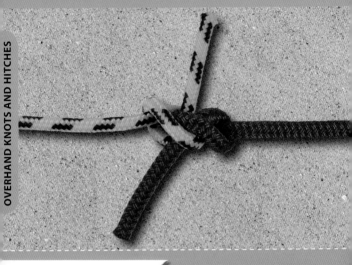

STEP-BY-STEP

① Take two ropes and lay them side by side. Form two interlocking loops, making sure that the loop on the right is twisted behind the loop on the left.

② Next, take the working end on the left side and bring it forward and down through both loops.

24

The hunter's bend is a versatile knot that can be used even with slippery synthetic rope. It is made up of two overhand knots that interlink to make one strong one. It is excellent for joining ropes together, but it does take a little practice, so be patient. Square in shape, the hunter's bend is primarily used in sailing, but climbers sometimes favor this knot too.

The hunter's bend found fame on the front page of the *London Times* in 1978, crediting Dr. Edward Hunter as the originator. Because of the article, the knot received a lot of publicity that resulted in the formation of the International Guild of Knot Tyers.

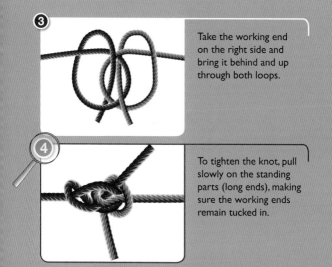

③ Take the working end on the right side and bring it behind and up through both loops.

④ To tighten the knot, pull slowly on the standing parts (long ends), making sure the working ends remain tucked in.

OVERHAND SHORTENING

STEP-BY-STEP

①

Fold your rope into three parts as shown here.

②

Using all three layers of the rope, start to tie an overhand knot.

There will probably be many occasions when a rope is too long for the job at hand, so knowing how to shorten a rope is valuable. There are a number of different knots for this purpose, many ornamental in appearance, but the overhand shortening knot is one of the simplest.

This method involves shortening the rope by folding it into three, and tying an overhand knot in the center to hold the parts firmly. The overhand knot is very secure, and provided you make sure that there are no twists in the rope, it will hold the three pieces together safely.

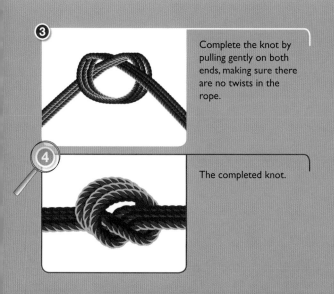

③ Complete the knot by pulling gently on both ends, making sure there are no twists in the rope.

④ The completed knot.

PERFECTION LOOP

STEP-BY-STEP

1 Tie a simple overhand knot and then pass the working end through the point of attachment.

2 Take the working end and pass it through the middle of the knot you have just made, creating a drawloop.

This is a popular knot because it can be tied through a ring and remains secure. It is the easiest way to tie a small loop that is perfectly in line with the standing part of a rope or line. The perfection loop (or angler's loop) can also be used to attach a rope to a mooring ring or other anchorage point, but it is essential to tie it with an end for this purpose.

The perfection loop, which is believed to date back to the 17th century, has been credited to Izaak Walton, the author of *The Compleat Angler,* although this has never been fully confirmed. It can be tied at speed, although it does have a tendency to jam in natural fiber ropes. It is a strong, secure knot, but bear in mind that once it is pulled tight it is almost impossible to untie, so only use it when a permanent knot is required.

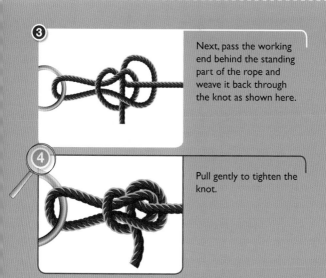

③ Next, pass the working end behind the standing part of the rope and weave it back through the knot as shown here.

④ Pull gently to tighten the knot.

REEF KNOT (SQUARE KNOT)

STEP-BY-STEP

1 Take two ropes. Hold the two ends of the ropes in each hand. Pass the left rope over the right rope and tuck under.

2 Now take the end in your right hand and lay it across the rope in your left hand.

This is an ancient knot that got its name from its use on sailing ships when sails were tied up or "reefed." It is popular with sailors because of the ease with which the knot can be released, simply by pulling the top end of the reef knot downwards, especially if they have only one hand free. It is the most common knot used to tie bootlaces, for which purpose most children are taught by using the simple chant:

Left over right and tuck under
Right over left and tuck under

Be aware that this knot can slip if it is used to tie two ropes of different thicknesses.

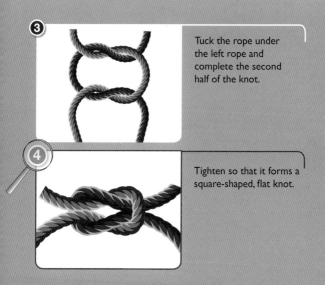

③ Tuck the rope under the left rope and complete the second half of the knot.

④ Tighten so that it forms a square-shaped, flat knot.

ROUND TURN & TWO HALF HITCHES

STEP-BY-STEP

① Pass the working end of the rope through the ring.

② Pass the working end of the rope through the ring for a second time.

A secure and simple knot, the round turn and two half hitches is used to secure a rope to a pole or ring. It is the ideal knot to start or finish a lashing, since the half hitches prevent the knot from unrolling because they have a locking effect. It will remain secure even if placed under a lot of strain—say, the movement of a boat or other weight—and yet it is simple to untie. Another advantage to this knot is that it will not slip along the object to which it is secured, which makes it useful in a variety of different situations.

For the purpose of this step-by-step sequence the rope is secured to a ring, rather than around a post.

③ Take the working end and place it over the top of the standing end. Bring the end upwards and through the loop that is formed.

④ Pull the first half hitch tight, then repeat, taking the working end over the top of the standing end, underneath, and through the loop.

⑤ Push the knot towards the ring to tighten and complete the knot.

TAUT-LINE HITCH

STEP-BY-STEP

1

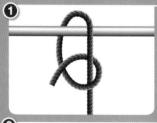

Pass the rope around the anchor object and then make a half hitch around the standing part of the rope.

2

Pass the working end over and around the standing part, then back through the loop formed in Step 1.

The taut-line hitch is ideal for creating adjustable moorings in tidal areas because it is a flexible loop for use on lines under tension. It is possible to maintain the tension by sliding the hitch to adjust the size of the loop without having to retie the knot. As this knot will only slide one way, it is most commonly used by campers to hold their guy ropes taut.

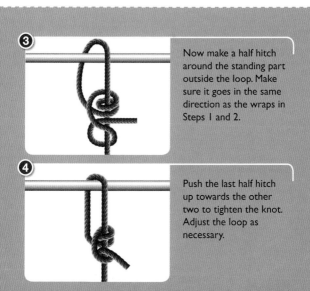

③ Now make a half hitch around the standing part outside the loop. Make sure it goes in the same direction as the wraps in Steps 1 and 2.

④ Push the last half hitch up towards the other two to tighten the knot. Adjust the loop as necessary.

ZEPPELIN BEND

STEP-BY-STEP

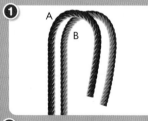

①

Take the two ropes to be joined (A and B) and bend the ends over as shown, with A lying on top of B and both working ends pointing in the same direction.

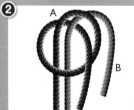

②

Using the working end of A, form an overhand loop that goes over both lines.

If you need to tie two ropes together, the Zeppelin bend is by far the best choice of knot because you can guarantee the ropes will not separate. The other advantage to this knot is that it will not jam and can be easily undone even if it has been subjected to a powerful force.

As the name suggests, this knot gets its name from the airships, or dirigibles, of the 1920s which were commonly called Zeppelins in honor of Count Ferdinand von Zeppelin. When filled with helium, these ships needed a secure mooring, so the ropes required a knot that could take a massive strain. The Zeppelin knot did just that and, although perhaps not so commonly used today, it is one that should be encouraged as it could definitely be classed as one of the best knots of all time.

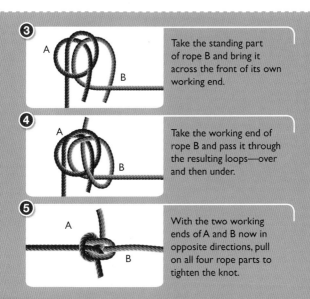

③ Take the standing part of rope B and bring it across the front of its own working end.

④ Take the working end of rope B and pass it through the resulting loops—over and then under.

⑤ With the two working ends of A and B now in opposite directions, pull on all four rope parts to tighten the knot.

FIGURE-OF-EIGHT KNOT

STEP-BY-STEP

① Take the working end of your rope and make an overhand loop.

② Give the loop a half twist by lifting the left-hand side of the loop over to the right-hand side.

Although this knot was discovered over 200 years ago, it is still the most frequently used stopper knot. The figure-of-eight knot was first identified after being recorded as the recommended knot for holding down sail sheets in *The Young Officer's Sheet Anchor* written by Darcy Lever.

It is as quick and easy to tie as it is to untie, and can easily be adapted to form a bend (see pages 40–41) or a hitch (see pages 42–43). It is a fairly stable knot, but be aware that it can come undone if it is subjected to a continuous swaying motion. It can be used in any situation where you need a line or rope to pass through a hole without slipping through or coming undone. This knot is a favorite with both sailors and climbers.

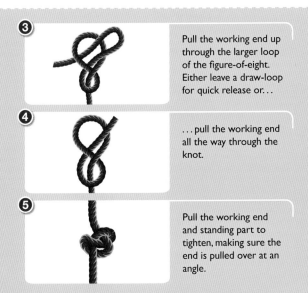

③ Pull the working end up through the larger loop of the figure-of-eight. Either leave a draw-loop for quick release or...

④ ...pull the working end all the way through the knot.

⑤ Pull the working end and standing part to tighten, making sure the end is pulled over at an angle.

FIGURE-OF-EIGHT BEND

STEP-BY-STEP

1 Take two pieces of rope and using the working end of one, tie a figure-of-eight knot around the other standing part.

2 Take the other working end and wrap it around the other standing part to form the first part of a figure-of-eight.

The figure-of-eight bend is a secure way to join two ropes together that are of light to medium weight. It can be used in many situations and is easy to untie even after it has been put under stress. The knot starts out with a simple figure-of-eight (see pages 38–39) tied around one of the ropes, which is repeated on the other rope to form a secure fixing.

It works extremely well with modern ropes, but can jam if you are using natural fiber ropes or cords.

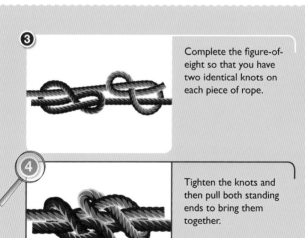

3

Complete the figure-of-eight so that you have two identical knots on each piece of rope.

4

Tighten the knots and then pull both standing ends to bring them together.

FIGURE-OF-EIGHT HITCH

STEP-BY-STEP

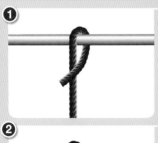

1 Pass the working end of your rope over the post and form a loop.

2 Bend the working end from right to left in front of the standing end and from left to right around the back.

The figure-of-eight hitch, a true general-purpose knot, is extremely simple and quick to tie. It forms a secure fixing to an immovable object but works best on posts, rails, or rings that are larger in diameter than the cord or rope being used. Its security comes from the fact that the working end twists back on itself, trapping it between the fixed object and the knot itself.

It is easy to untie but should be used with caution on nylon-based cords or ropes because it can slip. For demonstration purposes we are using a horizontal post.

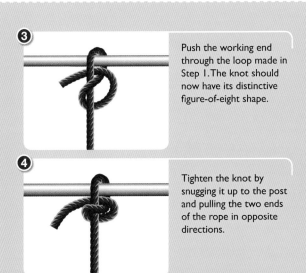

③ Push the working end through the loop made in Step 1. The knot should now have its distinctive figure-of-eight shape.

④ Tighten the knot by snugging it up to the post and pulling the two ends of the rope in opposite directions.

FLEMISH BEND

STEP-BY-STEP

1

Take the first line (red) and tie a figure-of-eight knot in the working end.

2

Introduce the blue line from the left by passing the working end through the left-most loop of the figure-of-eight formed above and parallel to the red line.

The Flemish bend went out of favor in the middle part of the 20th century because of its bulky nature and its tendency to jam when tied in ropes made of natural fiber. However, with the advent of modern synthetic ropes, this knot has made something of a comeback. It is a strong and reliable bend for joining two ropes or cords, which makes it very popular with climbers and sailors.

It is fairly simple to untie, especially when used with thicker lines, even if they have been subjected to considerable stress. To make a less bulky knot, make sure the two ropes swap sides each time they change direction.

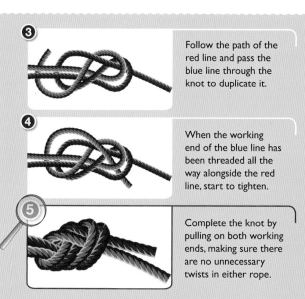

3 Follow the path of the red line and pass the blue line through the knot to duplicate it.

4 When the working end of the blue line has been threaded all the way alongside the red line, start to tighten.

5 Complete the knot by pulling on both working ends, making sure there are no unnecessary twists in either rope.

STEVEDORE'S KNOT

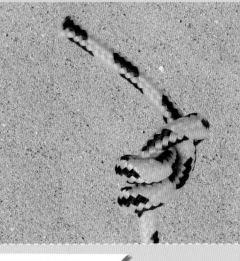

STEP-BY-STEP

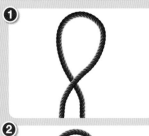

1 Make an overhand loop using one end of your working line.

2 Hold the loop and give it a half twist as if to tie a figure-of-eight knot.

Before the invention of cranes, longshoremen used the stevedore's knot for loading and unloading cargo from a ship's hold. They needed a powerful stopper knot to ensure that the rope didn't slip through the hoist pulley, and yet one that was easy to untie. The stevedore's knot was the perfect solution.

It is more bulky but less prone to jamming than the closely related figure-of-eight knot (see pages 38–39). Today its uses are less industrial, but it remains an excellent way of making sure that no line ever slips through a rope pulley. It can be tied in most types of line and also works well in thick rope. Although this knot is bulkier than the standard figure-of-eight, it can be untied more easily after use.

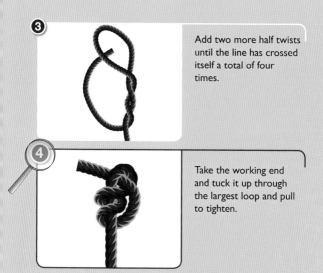

3 Add two more half twists until the line has crossed itself a total of four times.

4 Take the working end and tuck it up through the largest loop and pull to tighten.

BOWLINE

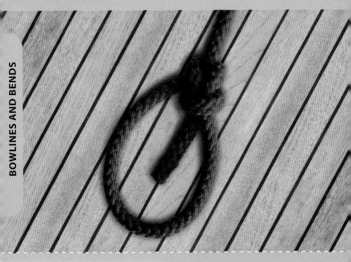

STEP-BY-STEP

1 Make a loop—a little over double the length you want the final loop to be.

2 Now bring the working end up through the loop.

The bowline is the most commonly used knot on a boat, because it holds fast when needed but is easy to release later. It's a very versatile knot that is quick to tie once you have the hang of it. It has many uses, such as fastening a mooring line to a ring or post. It is secure under load, since it doesn't slip or jam, but if there is no load on it, it is easy to untie. It is also useful if you want to join two ropes together.

The first reference to the bowline was in 1627 in a book written by John Smith called *Seaman's Grammar,* although many knot enthusiasts believe its history goes back much further to the ancient Egyptians.

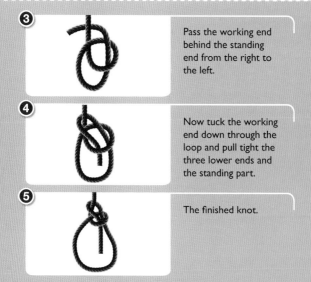

③ Pass the working end behind the standing end from the right to the left.

④ Now tuck the working end down through the loop and pull tight the three lower ends and the standing part.

⑤ The finished knot.

BOWLINE ON A BIGHT

STEP-BY-STEP

① Fold your rope in half and then make a small overhand loop in the doubled portion. Pass the end of the bight up through this loop.

② You now have two big loops. Open up the end of the doubled rope and bring it down and around in front of the two large loops.

The bowline on a bight is a double-loop variation of the basic bowline (see pages 48–49). It is a knot tied in the center of a line or rope when a loop is required and both ends are inaccessible. It makes a perfect improvised hoist if you have to lower or raise a sick or injured person, with one loop becoming the seat and the other going under the person's armpits and around their chest. It is important that the load should be applied equally to both standing loops.

Its advantages are that the loops do not slip and it is reasonably easy to untie after being exposed to strain.

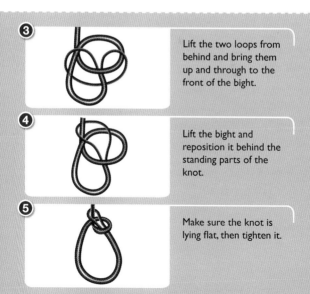

3 Lift the two loops from behind and bring them up and through to the front of the bight.

4 Lift the bight and reposition it behind the standing parts of the knot.

5 Make sure the knot is lying flat, then tighten it.

HEAVING-LINE BEND

STEP-BY-STEP

1

Make a loop in the heavier rope and lay the thinner line across it.

2

Next, take the working end of the thinner line behind the loop.

In the nautical world, bends have long been used to join heavier rope or cable to a thinner line. The heaving-line bend is used when you have a rope or cable that is too heavy to be thrown ashore or across an intervening gap on its own. It is pulled into position using a much lighter "heaving" line that is thrown ahead of the main rope.

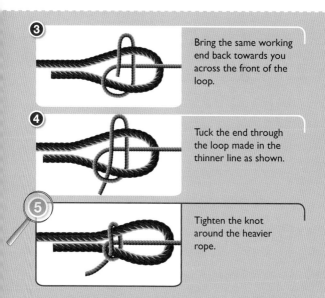

③ Bring the same working end back towards you across the front of the loop.

④ Tuck the end through the loop made in the thinner line as shown.

⑤ Tighten the knot around the heavier rope.

53

INUIT BOWLINE

STEP-BY-STEP

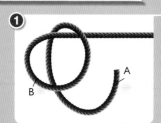

① Place the rope horizontally and make an overhand loop, bringing the working end (A) down behind loop B.

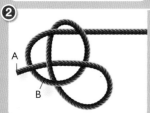

② Next, push the working end (A) through loop B by bringing A to the front, behind itself and then over the outer part of loop B as shown here.

Eskimo is a term for an Inuit, an indigenous person from North America and Greenland; for that reason, this knot is often mistakenly referred to as the Eskimo bowline. Its other name is the Boas bowline, after an American anthropologist by the name of Frank Boas, who recorded this knot being used by the Inuits of Baffin Island in 1907. Another reference to this early knot was made by the Arctic explorer Sir John Ross, who brought an Inuit sled back to England. On the sled the rawhide lashings were tied with this knot.

The Inuit knot has a fixed loop that makes it more secure than the common bowline, especially in synthetic lines. This knot is best used in situations where a loop is required at the end of a rope and in which the loop is going to be stretched wide.

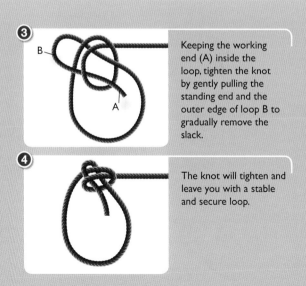

3

B —

A

Keeping the working end (A) inside the loop, tighten the knot by gently pulling the standing end and the outer edge of loop B to gradually remove the slack.

4

The knot will tighten and leave you with a stable and secure loop.

LAPP KNOT

STEP-BY-STEP

1 Make a bight in one end of the rope and lay the other working end diagonally across the top of the loop.

2 Tuck the working end down behind the loop.

Although the exact origin of the Lapp knot is not known, it was first documented as being used in 1892. It can be used as an alternative to a bowline and works well as an improvised safety line or tether.

The advantage of the Lapp knot is, if it is tied with a draw-loop, it becomes a quick-release knot. Unlike many other knots, the Lapp knot will fall apart with just one tug on the working end. This knot is also perfect for use as a curtain tie-back because it can be tied just as well with a short length of rope as a longer one.

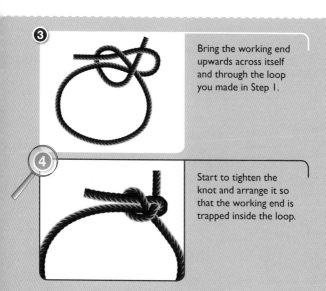

3 Bring the working end upwards across itself and through the loop you made in Step 1.

4 Start to tighten the knot and arrange it so that the working end is trapped inside the loop.

ROUND-TURN BOWLINE

STEP-BY-STEP

①

Make two overhand loops in the standing part of your rope.

②

Put the second loop on top of the first to form a round turn and then pass the working end up through the loops.

Bowline knots are used when you need a secure, non-slip loop at the end of a line, for example when mooring a boat or attaching a safety line. The round-turn bowline (often referred to as a double bowline) forms a more secure loop than the regular bowline. It also has an advantage over the figure-of-eight knot because it is easier to untie after the knot has been subjected to pressure.

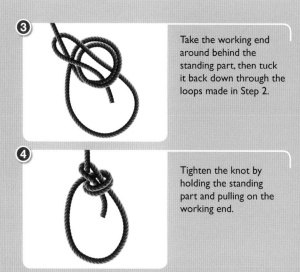

3 Take the working end around behind the standing part, then tuck it back down through the loops made in Step 2.

4 Tighten the knot by holding the standing part and pulling on the working end.

SHEET BEND

STEP-BY-STEP

1 Form a closed loop in the thicker rope and hold it in one hand.

2 Pass the thinner line through this loop and then around behind the thicker rope.

The sheet bend was first used in the late 18th century when sailors would quite literally "bend" one free end of a rope to another. It is a handy knot to know because it is used to join two ropes of different thicknesses without slipping. Its primary use was to secure the trimming ropes, or "sheets" as they were known, that were attached to the sails. This knot is also referred to as the flag bend since it was used to attach flags to masts.

If you are using lines that become slippery when wet, you can make this knot more secure by tying a "double" sheet bend. Simply add another round turn below the first and bring the working end back under itself as before. For maximum strength make sure both working ends are on the same side of the knot when completed.

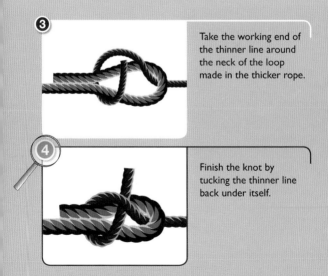

3

Take the working end of the thinner line around the neck of the loop made in the thicker rope.

4

Finish the knot by tucking the thinner line back under itself.

SIMPLE SIMON

STEP-BY-STEP

1 Take two pieces of rope and make a short bight (or closed loop) in one of them.

2 Tuck the working end of the other rope down through the original bight.

The simple simon knot was introduced by the late Harry Asher and first appeared in his book *A New System of Knotting*. This knot is a variation on the reef knot (see pages 30–31), but is tied in a totally different way by forming a bight in one rope and then threading the other rope through and around it to form the finished knot.

The advantage of this knot is that it is more secure than the reef knot and does not become loose or unravel if it's subjected to frequent jerking movements. It also holds well if it is tied using differently sized ropes, and even with synthetic ropes that tend to have less grip.

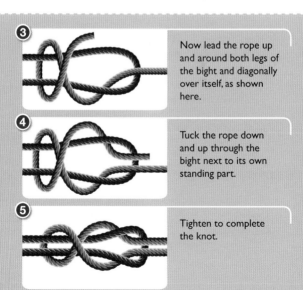

③ Now lead the rope up and around both legs of the bight and diagonally over itself, as shown here.

④ Tuck the rope down and up through the bight next to its own standing part.

⑤ Tighten to complete the knot.

TWIN BOWLINE BEND

STEP-BY-STEP

1 Lay two lines parallel to one another with their working ends pointing in opposite directions. Make a small overhand loop in one of the lines.

2 Take the working end from the other line and pass it up, around, down, and through the loop to form a bowline.

This is another bowline knot that can be used to join two ropes together, but this time they should be of a similar size and design. It is not as chunky as the regular bowline and is therefore less likely to catch on objects such as jagged rocks.

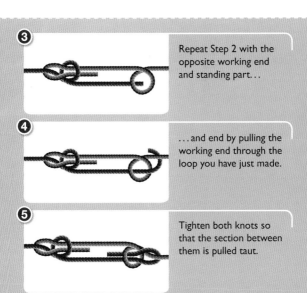

③ Repeat Step 2 with the opposite working end and standing part...

④ ...and end by pulling the working end through the loop you have just made.

⑤ Tighten both knots so that the section between them is pulled taut.

WATER BOWLINE

STEP-BY-STEP

① Make two overhand loops in the standing part of your rope. Pass the working end up through the loop closest to you.

② Continue threading the working end through the second loop and behind the standing part of the rope.

As the name suggests, the water bowline is designed for use in wet conditions where other knots may slip or jam. It is a very secure loop because the knot is formed using a clove hitch, which puts the working end through a doubled loop. Unlike most other knots, the water bowline will not change dramatically when underwater.

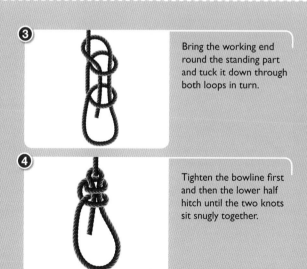

3 Bring the working end round the standing part and tuck it down through both loops in turn.

4 Tighten the bowline first and then the lower half hitch until the two knots sit snugly together.

CLOVE HITCH IN THE BIGHT

STEP-BY-STEP

1 Form an overhand loop in the bight.

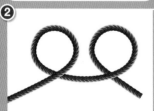

2 Make a second loop to the left of the first one as shown here.

The clove hitch, which has been around since the 18th century, was frequently used on square-rigged ships, particularly for the rope ladders that enabled sailors to reach the upper masts. The main aim of the clove hitch is to fasten a line at its midpoint, but it is not very secure and has a tendency to slip or jam. This knot works best with natural fiber rope rather than the more modern synthetic ones, as it can work loose on slippery surfaces.

The clove hitch can be tied in two ways, but when you need a knot that can be slipped over a post, or onto the end of a rail or spar, it is faster and simpler to tie it in the bight (i.e. in the middle).

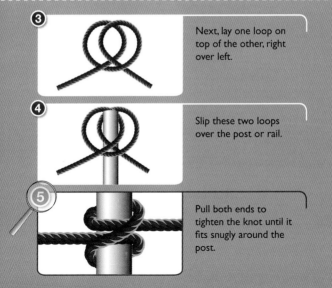

③ Next, lay one loop on top of the other, right over left.

④ Slip these two loops over the post or rail.

⑤ Pull both ends to tighten the knot until it fits snugly around the post.

GROUND-LINE HITCH

STEP-BY-STEP

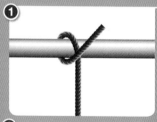

1 Wind the rope around the hitching post. Cross the line over the top of itself diagonally, working from left to right.

2 Take the working end behind the post again.

70

The ground-line hitch is more secure than the clove hitch when attaching a rope to an anchor point. It has less tendency to jam and stays secure if subjected to a swinging motion. It got its name from fishermen who used this knot to attach a net to the "groundline," which was a weighted rope on the bottom of the net. It has also been used by soldiers to tether their mounts, so it has been proven to be a reliable, strong knot.

The ground-line hitch works just as well in rope or flat webbing. It is also the most common knot for tying fender lines to guardrails.

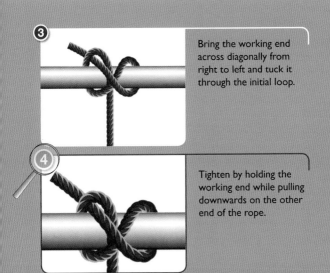

③ Bring the working end across diagonally from right to left and tuck it through the initial loop.

④ Tighten by holding the working end while pulling downwards on the other end of the rope.

MIDSHIPMAN'S HITCH

STEP-BY-STEP

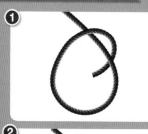

① Form an overhand loop in the end of your rope and bring the working end through from back to front.

② Take the working end up and over the standing part, forming a diagonal, wrapping turn.

The midshipman's hitch is an excellent knot used primarily for moorings or for providing tension on guy lines, since it creates an adjustable, strong, secure loop. It has, however, also been used as a rescue line for people who have fallen into the water, because it will remain firm while they are pulled to safety. As it is possible to slide the knot to a new position and still hold firm, it is perfect for tying bales or parcels.

The downside to this knot is that it may not work well on especially stiff or slippery rope, and it is essential that it be pulled tight to work efficiently.

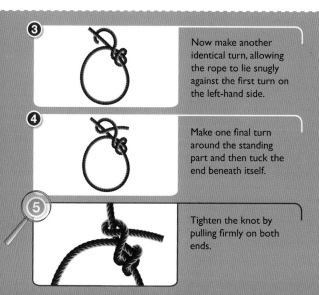

3 Now make another identical turn, allowing the rope to lie snugly against the first turn on the left-hand side.

4 Make one final turn around the standing part and then tuck the end beneath itself.

5 Tighten the knot by pulling firmly on both ends.

ROLLING HITCH

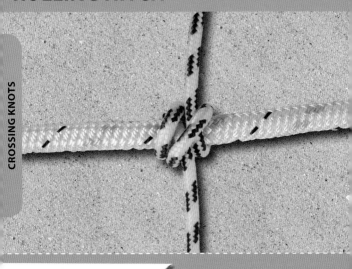

STEP-BY-STEP

1 Pass the working end of your thinner line over the thicker static rope and wrap it around. Allow it to cross over its own standing part.

2 Bring the working end down behind, then take it up diagonally from left to right. Let it cross over and trap its own standing part.

The rolling hitch, like many of the knots in this book, dates back to the 18th century when it was widely used at sea. It is recognized for its ability to withstand strain, although it is more reliable when tied in natural fiber ropes than synthetic varieties. One of its most practical uses is for exerting force along another line. If, for instance, a jib sheet were to jam in a winch, you could attach a rolling hitch to help take the pressure off the line while you work to undo the jam.

If you are using this knot to attach a line to a rail, post, or spar, it is essential, for it to remain secure, that the pull comes from the side of the knot that has the two diagonal turns against the standing part.

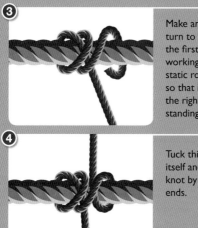

3 Make another diagonal turn to the right of the first one. Take the working end behind the static rope once more so that it comes out on the right-hand side of the standing part.

4 Tuck this end up beneath itself and tighten the knot by pulling on both ends.

POLE LASHING

STEP-BY-STEP

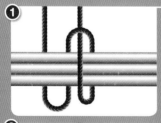

Forming an S shape, lay your rope underneath one end of the items to be tied together.

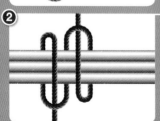

Tuck each of the working ends through its opposite bight or loop.

This is an invaluable knot for tying together an awkward bundle of differently sized objects; it's especially useful if you don't want them to roll around on the deck in rough weather.

It can also be used as a clamp while nailing or glueing something in place. The hitch is formed in two parts, but it is still quick to tie and will hold firmly once tightened.

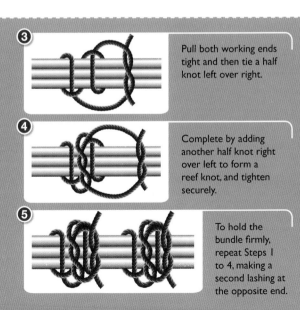

3 Pull both working ends tight and then tie a half knot left over right.

4 Complete by adding another half knot right over left to form a reef knot, and tighten securely.

5 To hold the bundle firmly, repeat Steps 1 to 4, making a second lashing at the opposite end.

SAILOR'S GRIPPING HITCH

STEP-BY-STEP

1 Make five turns around your object in the opposite direction to the pull.

2 Make another turn and bring the working end in front of the standing part so that it is facing in the opposite direction.

The sailor's gripping hitch is a knot that allows a lengthwise pull on a smooth spar, rope, pole, boom, or such. It is very easy to tie and will even handle tapered objects such as a marlin spike, as long as the pull is in the direction of the taper.

This hitch works best if the pull is steady and constant, but if you want to increase the grip you can place a small piece of rubber beneath the knot. It can also be used to tie one rope to another, even if they are of different thicknesses.

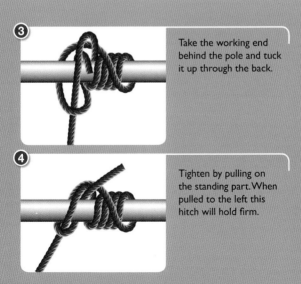

3

Take the working end behind the pole and tuck it up through the back.

4

Tighten by pulling on the standing part. When pulled to the left this hitch will hold firm.

SNUGGLE HITCH

STEP-BY-STEP

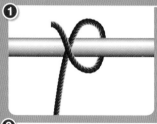

① Wrap the line around your anchor point and bring the working end across diagonally from right to left over the standing part.

② Take the working end back over the anchor point and bring it up behind, crossing over diagonally from left to right. Tuck it up through the first loop you made.

The inventor of this knot was Owen K. Nuttall of the International Guild of Knot Tyers in 1987. It is a modification of the clove hitch, but far stronger and more secure. It is useful for attaching a line to a spar or rope, and can be used for either a lengthways or right-angled pull. Its value is that it can be tied either in the end of the rope or in the bight, and is easy to release.

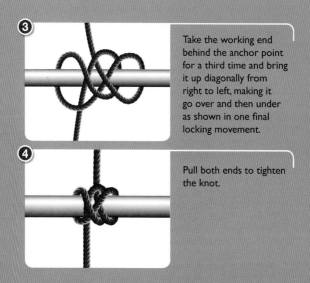

3 Take the working end behind the anchor point for a third time and bring it up diagonally from right to left, making it go over and then under as shown in one final locking movement.

4 Pull both ends to tighten the knot.

ANGLER'S LOOP

STEP-BY-STEP

1 To start, hold the rope in both hands (the end in the right hand should be the shorter one). Now make an under-hand loop.

2 Wrap the working end in front of the loop you have just made. Bring it down again behind the standing end.

The angler's loop is a simple way of tying a loop in the end of a line, which is easy to release. Originally it was designed to be tied in monofilament fishing line, but it is also useful when you need to throw a rope over an item such as a post (to tie up a boat or when you need to attach something to a loop of rope, for example).

It fell out of favor with sailors because it tended to jam in ropes made of natural fiber, but this problem has largely been solved with the use of modern synthetic ropes. It is a strong, secure knot, but the drawback is that it is extremely difficult to undo once pulled tight.

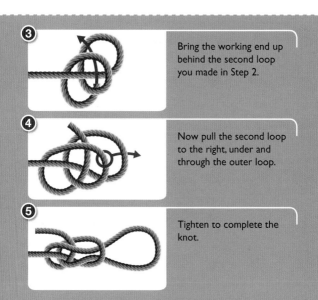

3 Bring the working end up behind the second loop you made in Step 2.

4 Now pull the second loop to the right, under and through the outer loop.

5 Tighten to complete the knot.

COMMON ROPE SEIZING

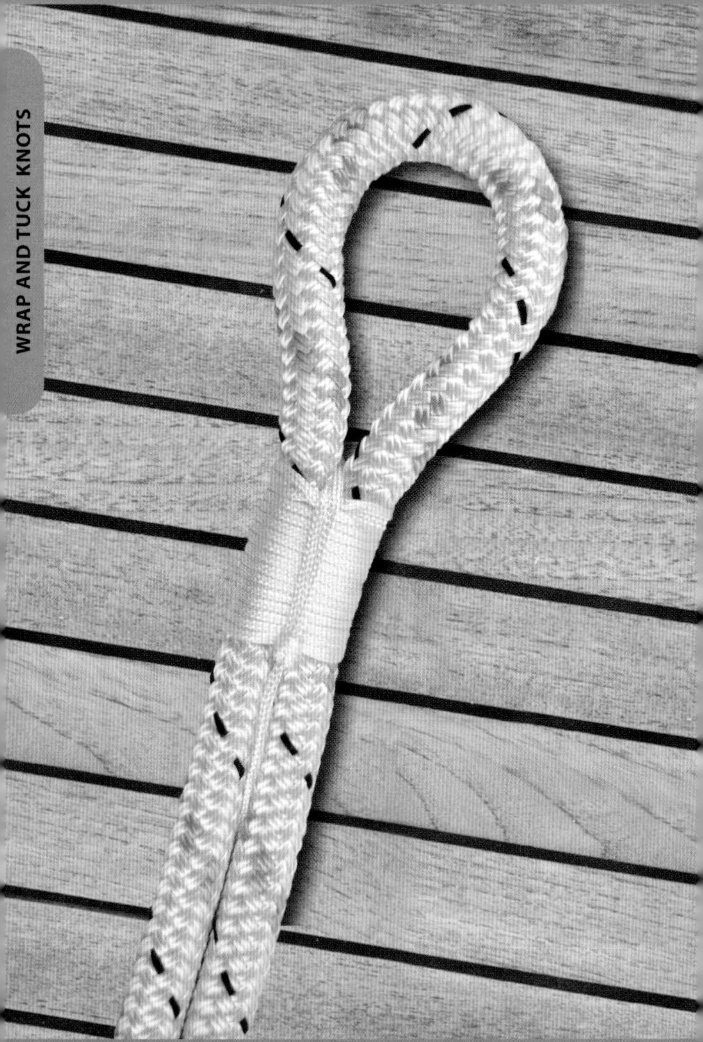

Rope seizing is a technique that is used when you want to hold two pieces of rope together using cord. It is a good alternative to knotting, although not quite as strong as splicing (which is when you join two ropes together by partially unravelling and then intertwining the strands). A common seizing is generally used to join two parallel sections of rope or, as in this example, to make an eye in a rope.

STEP-BY-STEP

1 Make a closed loop in your rope. Bind the two pieces together with cord by first tying a clove hitch (see pages 68–69).

2 Using the working end of the cord, start to make a series of tightly wrapped turns. Make sure they sit neatly next to one another.

COMMON ROPE SEIZING

WRAP AND TUCK KNOTS

③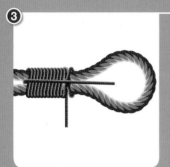

Continue making turns until you have at least 12, or about three times the width of the final seizing desired. On the last turn, only wrap the cord around one section of the rope and bring the working end up between the two sections of the rope.

④

Tuck the working end down through the loop, around the back and up between the two sections of the rope once more to form a tight binding.

⑤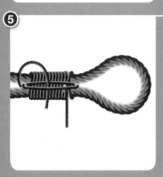

Repeat this once more—these are called "frapping turns." Next, tuck the working end down through the middle of the two frapping turns, taking it from the top to the bottom as shown here.

6

Take the working end up and behind the two frapping turns and bring it out in the middle of the two frapping turns.

7

Finally, pull the working end tight, which creates a square knot in the seizing in the middle of the two legs of the rope. Trim off the excess from the two ends of cord.

COMMON WHIPPING

STEP-BY-STEP

1 Make a fairly long, closed loop in the whipping twine and lay it over the top of the rope with the top of the loop facing the standing part of the rope.

2 Using the working end, start to make a series of tight wraps around the rope to trap the loop in place.

Common whipping is a way of preventing the ends of rope from fraying or unravelling. Ideally, when whipping any rope you should use a specially prepared waxed whipping twine, as this will give you better purchase on the rope itself. We have used a cord thicker than regular whipping twine for this example, so that you can see the steps more clearly.

This is the most basic form of whipping, but it does have the disadvantage of slipping off the end if the rope is handled frequently. The advantage, however, is that no special tools are required. In general, it is only natural fiber ropes that need whipping; the artificial fiber ropes usually have their ends fused by heat.

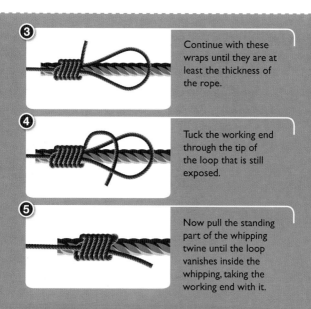

③ Continue with these wraps until they are at least the thickness of the rope.

④ Tuck the working end through the tip of the loop that is still exposed.

⑤ Now pull the standing part of the whipping twine until the loop vanishes inside the whipping, taking the working end with it.

CONSTRICTOR KNOT

STEP-BY-STEP

1 Wrap the twine around the end of the rope.

2 Tie a clove hitch (see pages 68–69).

The constrictor knot was first mentioned in 1944 in *The Ashley Book of Knots*, but it is thought to date back much further. It is one of the most effective binding knots because it grips tightly, just like the boa constrictor which gives it its name. It is an excellent, quick way of temporarily stopping the ends of a rope from fraying, securely tying the neck of a sack or bag, or for holding items together that need glueing.

The other advantages of this knot are that it can be tied very quickly and it binds so well that it is almost impossible to undo. Its weakness is that it does not work well when tied on a flat surface: it needs a curved surface to grip. It can, however, be tied either in the end of a rope or on the bight, and is normally tied in twine.

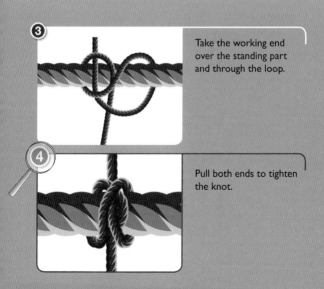

3 Take the working end over the standing part and through the loop.

4 Pull both ends to tighten the knot.

HEAVING LINE KNOT

STEP-BY-STEP

1

Fold your rope into three parts.

2

Tuck the working end from right to left —under, then over— and out through the adjacent loop.

Occasionally, you need to get a line ashore or across to another boat, and this is where you would use the heaving line knot. Because it is impossible to throw a piece of rope any distance unless it is properly prepared, using this knot on the end of the rope adds bulk and weight, making it easier to throw.

There are many variations to this knot, but this is a simple version that is commonly used in sailing (or for tying the ends of a monk's rope belt!).

3 Now wrap the working end tightly, counter-clockwise, around both the legs of the two loops. Make another wrap, but this time include all three legs to draw them together.

4 Continue with more tight wraps until you reach the bottom end of the bight. On your final wrap, tuck the working end through the bottom of the bight.

5 Pull the standing part to tighten.

JACK KETCH'S KNOT

STEP-BY-STEP

1

Fold the rope into three parts.

2

Using the working end, make two tight wrapping turns around all three parts of the rope.

3

Continue to make turns.

This knot was named after an infamous executioner employed by Charles II. Also known as the hangman's knot or hangman's noose because of its rather macabre past, today this knot makes a strong and useful general-purpose loop. The number of wraps depends entirely on its intended use and the type and thickness of the rope being used. If you are using natural fiber ropes, then six to eight loops are generally sufficient.

This knot is often used by sailors to secure an eyelet onto a rope or sheet without the need for splicing. It is also frequently used by lure fishermen to attach their line to the lure's towing eyelet.

④ Stop when you have made at least six wraps, enclosing the three rope parts in a neat bunch.

⑤ Tuck the working end through the loop exposed on the right-hand side.

⑥ Pull the loop leg on the left-hand side to bring the right-hand loop inside the wraps, making sure the working end is trapped tightly.

PERFECTED WHIPPING

Perfected whipping is another excellent way of preventing the ends of a rope from fraying or unravelling. Once again it is best to use waxed twine, which should be wound as tightly as possible.

One thing to note is that during the wrapping the loop itself will twist, which makes the tightening of the whipping very difficult. To avoid this, remember to twist the right-hand trapped end clockwise, to insert a few deliberate twists in the working loop before you start. Because they are twisted in the opposite direction to the ones the loop will make, they gradually disappear as you wrap.

STEP-BY-STEP

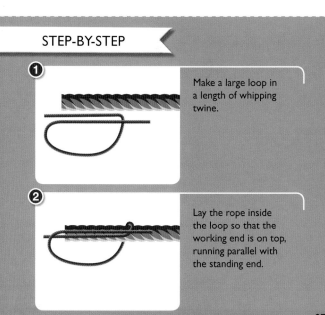

① Make a large loop in a length of whipping twine.

② Lay the rope inside the loop so that the working end is on top, running parallel with the standing end.

PERFECTED WHIPPING

③

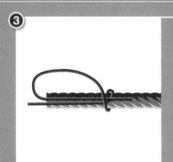

Using the large loop, start to wrap it around the rope, making sure that the twine lies flat by twisting as you go.

④

As you twist the twine around the rope make sure to trap both the working and the standing ends.

⑤

Make another turn with the loop, ensuring that the turns sit snugly up against one another without any twists. You may need to untangle the standing end from the unused portion of the loop.

6

Continue wrapping in the same way, making sure that the twine doesn't become twisted.

7

When the whipping has reached the required length—at least the width of the rope—pull on the right-hand side so that the remaining part of the loop is pulled into the wraps.

8

Pull on both ends to tighten the whipping fully.

SCAFFOLD KNOT

STEP-BY-STEP

1 Make a closed loop in one end of the rope. Take the working end down and around the neck of the loop.

2 Wrap the working end down, around, and behind the loop as before (twice).

The scaffold knot is a popular marine knot that can also be used for search and rescue, mountaineering, climbing, boating, horses and livestock, camping and scouting.

This is a good strong knot that is fairly simple to tie. Favored by fishermen for tying their line to a hook, this knot produces a sliding loop that can be undone easily by tugging on the standing part.

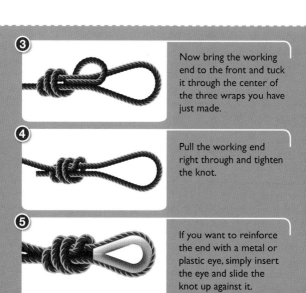

3 Now bring the working end to the front and tuck it through the center of the three wraps you have just made.

4 Pull the working end right through and tighten the knot.

5 If you want to reinforce the end with a metal or plastic eye, simply insert the eye and slide the knot up against it.

TRIPLE FISHERMAN'S KNOT

STEP-BY-STEP

1

Lie the two lines parallel with one another, with their ends facing in opposite directions. Tie a triple overhand knot in the red line (see pages 16–17) with one working end around the standing part of the blue line. Then begin to tie an identical knot in the blue line.

Just like the fisherman's knot (see pages 22–23), the double or triple fisherman's knot is used to connect two ropes. It is very popular with climbers and anglers because the extra turns give it additional security.

The triple version shown here is also known as the double grapevine or double grinner knot, and it can be relied upon to cope with a heavy workload. Anglers favor this knot for joining lengths of fishing line, although it should not be used on ropes that differ greatly in diameter. The greater the difference, the weaker the knot will be.

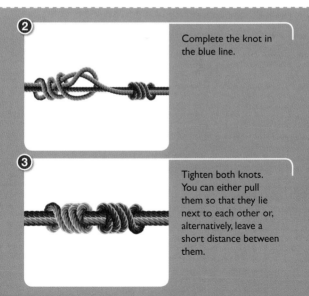

② Complete the knot in the blue line.

③ Tighten both knots. You can either pull them so that they lie next to each other or, alternatively, leave a short distance between them.

ALPINE BUTTERFLY

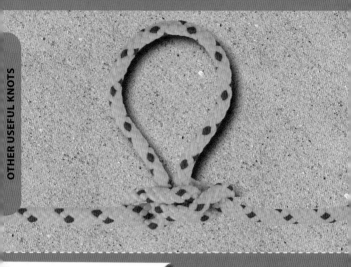

STEP-BY-STEP

①

Make an overhand loop in the rope at the point where you want to tie the knot.

②

Take hold of the top of the loop and twist it to the right so that it resembles a figure-of-eight.

This useful knot, thought to have been invented by mountaineers over a century ago, was used to attach the climber to the middle of a rope. Today it has other uses because it retains an extraordinary strength even when pulled in different directions.

The alpine butterfly can be used in any situation where you need a secure loop in the middle of a rope. Although harder to tie, it is much more secure than the bowline on a bight (see pages 50–51). It is suitable for virtually any type of rope or line and is easy to untie unless it becomes too wet.

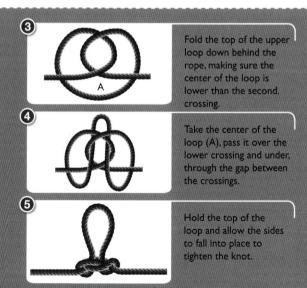

3 Fold the top of the upper loop down behind the rope, making sure the center of the loop is lower than the second crossing.

4 Take the center of the loop (A), pass it over the lower crossing and under, through the gap between the crossings.

5 Hold the top of the loop and allow the sides to fall into place to tighten the knot.

CARRICK BEND

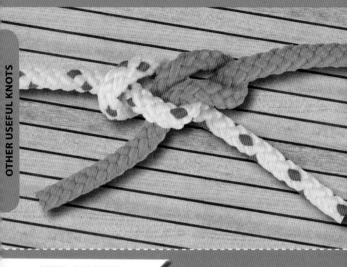

STEP-BY-STEP

1

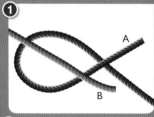

Make an overhand loop in one of the ropes (A) and then lay the other one (B) across it.

2

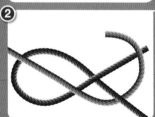

Next, take B under the standing part of A and over the working end of A.

The carrick bend is an ancient nautical knot that was used to join two large hawsers together. This knot is probably the nearest you will get to a perfect bend when joining heavy ropes, even ones of slightly differing thicknesses. It is symmetrical, easy to tie, and exceptionally strong. It will not slip or jam, and yet it is still easy to untie even after it has been under pressure.

You will find that when the strain is taken on the end, this knot will actually tighten and collapse on itself. It is important to make sure that both working ends are on the same side of the completed knot.

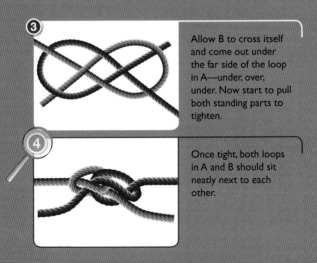

③ Allow B to cross itself and come out under the far side of the loop in A—under, over, under. Now start to pull both standing parts to tighten.

④ Once tight, both loops in A and B should sit neatly next to each other.

CATSPAW

STEP-BY-STEP

①

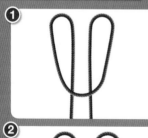

Make a bight (or loop) in the rope and allow it to drop forward to form two loops.

②

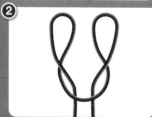

Next, twist the left-hand loop clockwise and the right-hand loop counter-clockwise.

The catspaw is a secure hitch that is used to fasten a sling to a hook or bar so that it can be lifted safely. The knot is formed by twisting two loops and slipping them over the end of the bar or hook.

This knot, thought to have been invented by the ancient Greeks, has enjoyed a revival in recent years. It is popular with lure and fly fishermen who use it to attach a line to a swivel. It can be used with a wide variety of lines or ropes of almost any size.

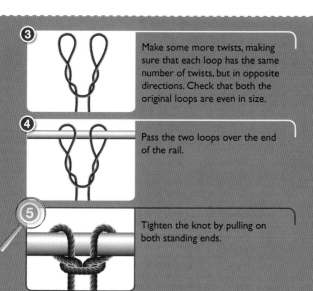

③ Make some more twists, making sure that each loop has the same number of twists, but in opposite directions. Check that both the original loops are even in size.

④ Pass the two loops over the end of the rail.

⑤ Tighten the knot by pulling on both standing ends.

HALYARD HITCH

STEP-BY-STEP

1 Wrap the working end of your rope around the anchor point twice.

2 Take it around one more time, but this time bring the working end around behind the standing part.

The halyard hitch is another ancient nautical knot that is typically used for securing spars. It is easy to tie, very neat, and holds effectively under load.

In sailing, the term "halyard" (or "halliard") comes from the phrase "to haul yards." It is, quite simply, a rope that is used to hoist a sail or flag. Traditionally, halyards would have been made from a natural fiber such as hemp or manila.

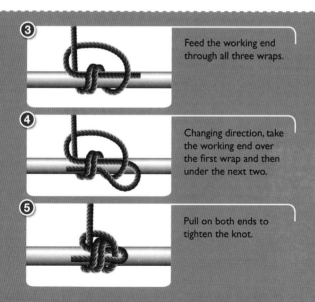

③ Feed the working end through all three wraps.

④ Changing direction, take the working end over the first wrap and then under the next two.

⑤ Pull on both ends to tighten the knot.

JURY MAST KNOT

STEP-BY-STEP

1 Make three overhand loops, with the center one the largest. Overlap the edges of the loops —right over middle, middle over left.

2 Push the loops closer together until the inner edge of the left-hand loop overlaps the inner edge of the right-hand loop.

Traditionally used for rigging a temporary jury mast on a boat or ship when the original mast was damaged or lost, this knot was placed at the top of the new mast, which projected from the middle of the knot. The loops were used as anchor points for makeshift stays. As the knot didn't actually grab the mast, it was necessary to hold it in place, and for that reason it is little used today except as decoration or to rig a mast on a yacht's tender.

This knot is also referred to as the pitcher knot, since it was once used to make handles for earthenware pitchers and bottles. If used for this purpose, the center of the knot acts as the base, while the loops are usually whipped close to the top of the pitcher to form the handles. Used for this purpose, the knot can withstand quite heavy loads.

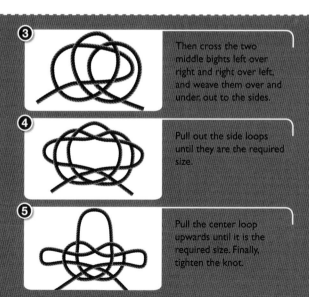

③ Then cross the two middle bights left over right and right over left, and weave them over and under, out to the sides.

④ Pull out the side loops until they are the required size.

⑤ Pull the center loop upwards until it is the required size. Finally, tighten the knot.

KNUTE KNOT

STEP-BY-STEP

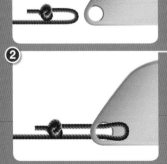

1

To make the knot more secure, tie a figure-of-eight as a stopper knot in the working end. Then, make a small loop in the cord, making sure that it will go through the hole in the tool when doubled.

2

Next, pass the loop through the hole in the tool.

This tiny yet very simple knot is invaluable when working on on a boat, and has no doubt saved many small objects from being lost overboard. Also, when working on anything above deck level, all tools should be fitted with a lanyard to prevent their falling into the water or hurting someone below. It also saves a lot of energy because the sailor doesn't have to climb down again should he drop the tool.

When using the knute knot, make sure the diameter of the rope is no less than half the size of the hole in the tool.

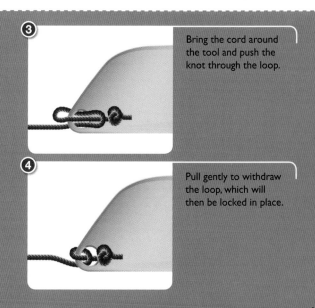

3 Bring the cord around the tool and push the knot through the loop.

4 Pull gently to withdraw the loop, which will then be locked in place.

LIGHTERMAN'S HITCH

Originally the lighterman's hitch was used by the Thames lightermen, who carried freight down the river on engineless barges. Today it is used to moor any vessel to a bollard, as it holds firm without slipping or jamming.

The greatest advantage of this hitch is that it is exceptionally quick to tie and can be released in seconds, even if there's a current to contend with. When tying this knot you need to make sure that you have a long working end and that the top of the hitching post is accessible.

STEP-BY-STEP

①

Wrap the working end of your rope around the hitching post twice, to provide sufficient friction to withstand the load.

②

Next, form a loop in the working end.

LIGHTERMAN'S HITCH

③ Now pass the loop underneath the standing part of the rope.

④ Lift the loop and drop it over the top of the post and pull on the working end to close the loop.

⑤ Starting from the opposite side of the standing part, wrap the working part of the rope over the top of the post.

6

Once the rope is over the top of the post, pull to tighten.

7

Take the working end over the top of the standing part, forming a loop around it. Take one final turn around the post and allow the end to hang loosely.

MONKEY'S FIST

STEP-BY-STEP

① Take the working end of your rope and make three circular turns.

② Change direction by turning the rope at right angles and make three circular turns around the first loops. Now you have a kind of core if you wish to insert a weight of some kind in the center.

The monkey's fist is a fascinating knot with a long history. It was originally used by sailors to throw a rope from one boat to another in an emergency. The knot on the end of the line gave it extra weight that helped to project it through the air towards the other vessel (acting as a heaving line). Today, it is more commonly used as a fancy knot for necklaces, earrings, keyrings, bellpulls, or other decorative items.

This knot can be tied with or without a central core (for example, a round stone). A heavy core gives an extra bit of weight at the end of the rope.

③

Next, turn the rope at right angles again and circle the second set of loops, but this time passing the rope around inside the original set of loops. At this point the fist is complete but needs to be tightened.

④

To tighten the monkey's fist, don't simply pull on both ends—rather, you will need to pull each part of the wrapping until it becomes snug around the central core.

MOORING HITCH

STEP-BY-STEP

1 Pass the end of your rope through the fixing ring and form a clockwise underhand loop.

2 Make sure the loop goes over the standing part.

The mooring hitch is a simple, quick-release knot that can be used for a temporary mooring. It can be released without even having to leave the boat, by simply giving a quick pull on the working end, and yet it will hold fast while under tension.

However, the mooring hitch is only intended as a temporary fixture so it should not be relied upon if you are going to leave your vessel unattended.

③ Form a small bight in the working end and weave it across the loop, going under the standing part and coming out on top of the loop. This part forms the locking draw-loop, which allows the knot to be released quickly.

④ Tighten to complete the knot.

OSSEL KNOT

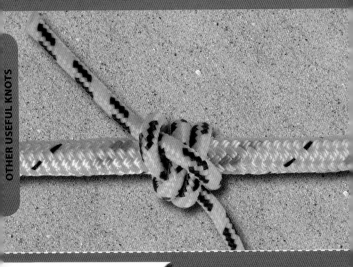

STEP-BY-STEP

1 Take the working end of your cord over and behind the main rope.

2 Bring it up diagonally in front of the standing part and behind the main rope again.

The ossel knot is a hitch that is most often used at sea to tie a smaller line to a larger one. It is relatively easy to tie and is able to withstand severe weather conditions when afloat. Traditionally this knot was used to secure the support ropes attaching drift nets to the headrope. The word *ossel* comes from the Scottish word *norsel*, which was a fisherman's term for a gill net.

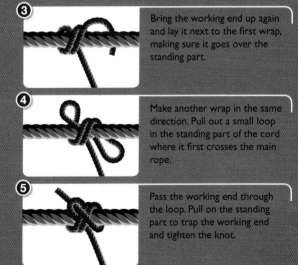

③ Bring the working end up again and lay it next to the first wrap, making sure it goes over the standing part.

④ Make another wrap in the same direction. Pull out a small loop in the standing part of the cord where it first crosses the main rope.

⑤ Pass the working end through the loop. Pull on the standing part to trap the working end and tighten the knot.

POST HITCH

STEP-BY-STEP

① Make a loop in the end of the rope.

② Pass the loop around the post and out underneath the two standing parts.

The post hitch, also known as the double pile hitch, is used to secure a line around a post or pile. It is most commonly used to moor a boat to a pile on the dock. It is also a very useful knot for campers, because it can secure a tent flap to a post to stop it from flapping around in the wind. It is quick to tie, holds securely, and is easy to untie.

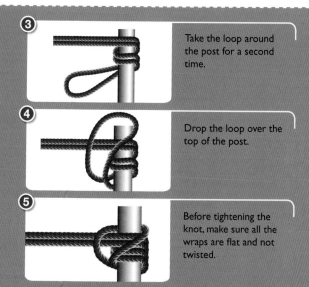

③ Take the loop around the post for a second time.

④ Drop the loop over the top of the post.

⑤ Before tightening the knot, make sure all the wraps are flat and not twisted.

INDEX